This book belongs to:

....

....

Copyright ©2024 by Arona Gallery

All rights reserved. No part of this publication may be reproduced, distributed, or transmitted in any form or by any means, including photocopying, recording, or other electronic or mechanical methods, without the prior written permission of the publisher, except in the case of brief quotations embodied in critical reviews and certain other noncommercial uses permitted by copyright law.

I SPY WITH MY LITTLE EYES...

1 white rabbit

2 yellow ducks

3 brown horses

4 pink pigs

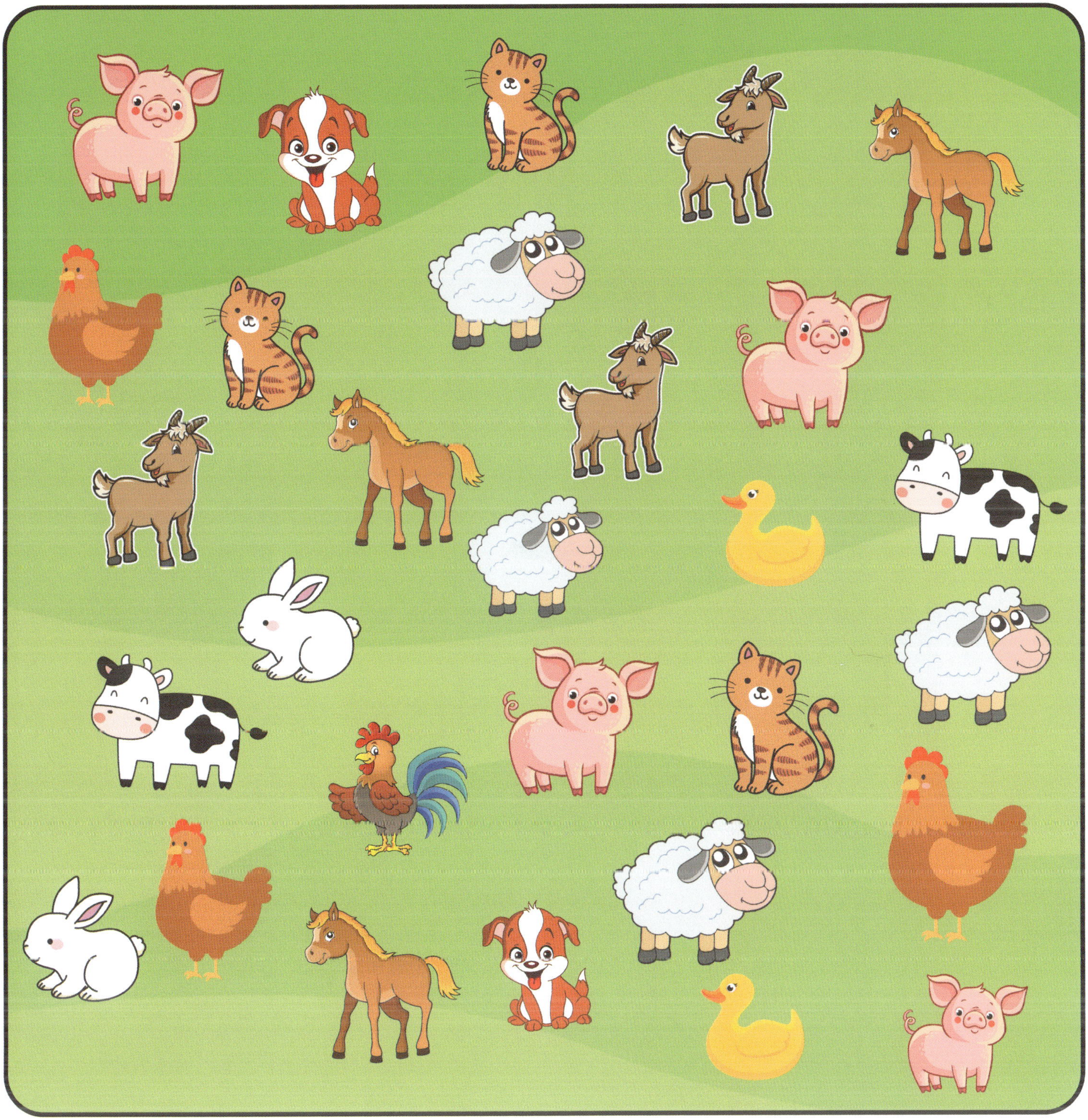

I SPY WITH MY LITTLE EYES...

4 red cars

5 blue boats

3 yellow cabs

1 white ambulance

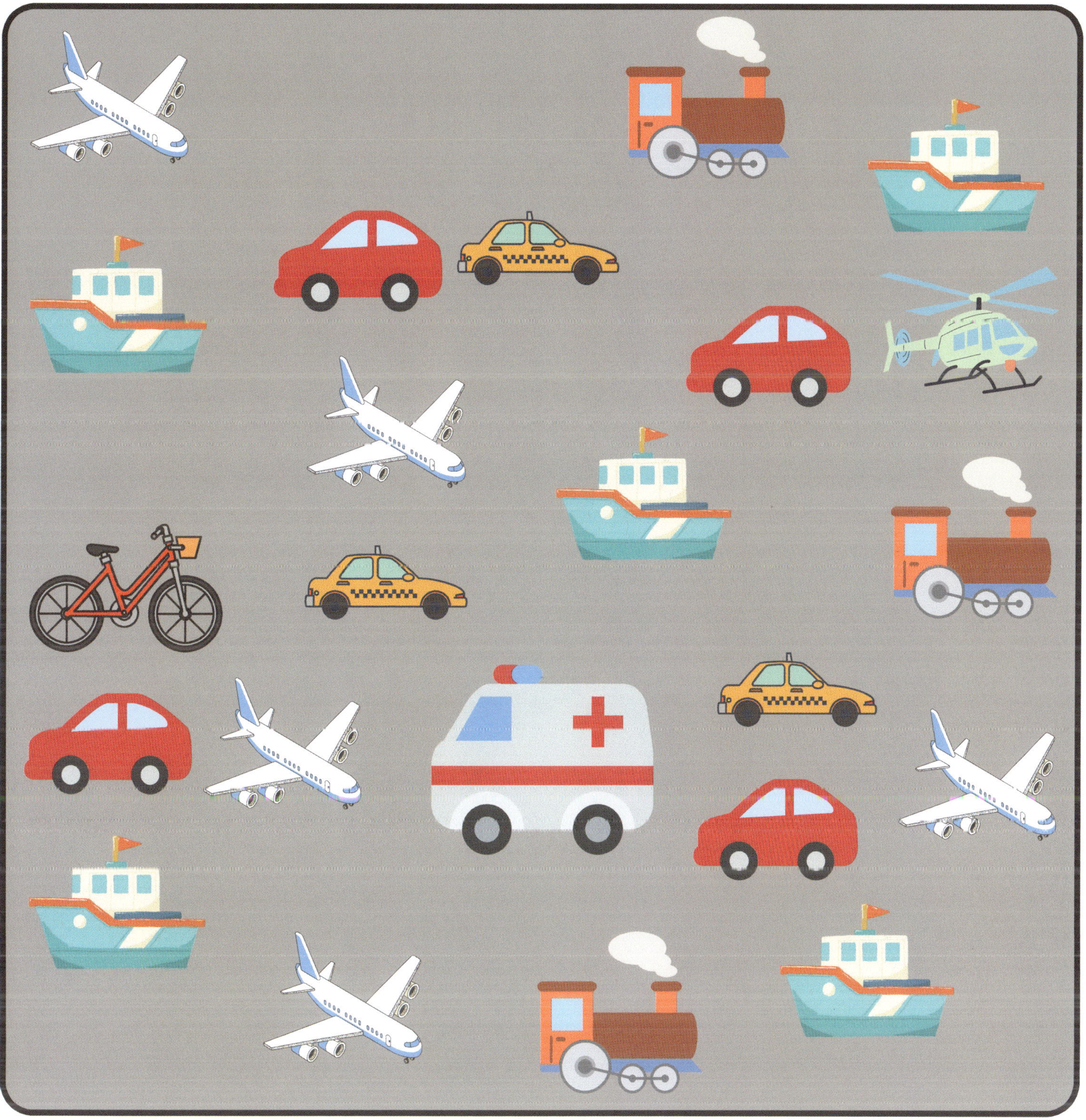

I SPY WITH MY LITTLE EYES...

2 **orange pufferfish**

3 **blue dolphins**

5 **pink squid**

6 **yellow starfish**

I SPY WITH MY LITTLE EYES SOMETHING BEGINNING WITH ...

F

Present

Tree

Duck

Ball

Heart

Leaf

Flower

Bow

Hat

I SPY WITH MY LITTLE EYES SOMETHING BEGINNING WITH ...

F

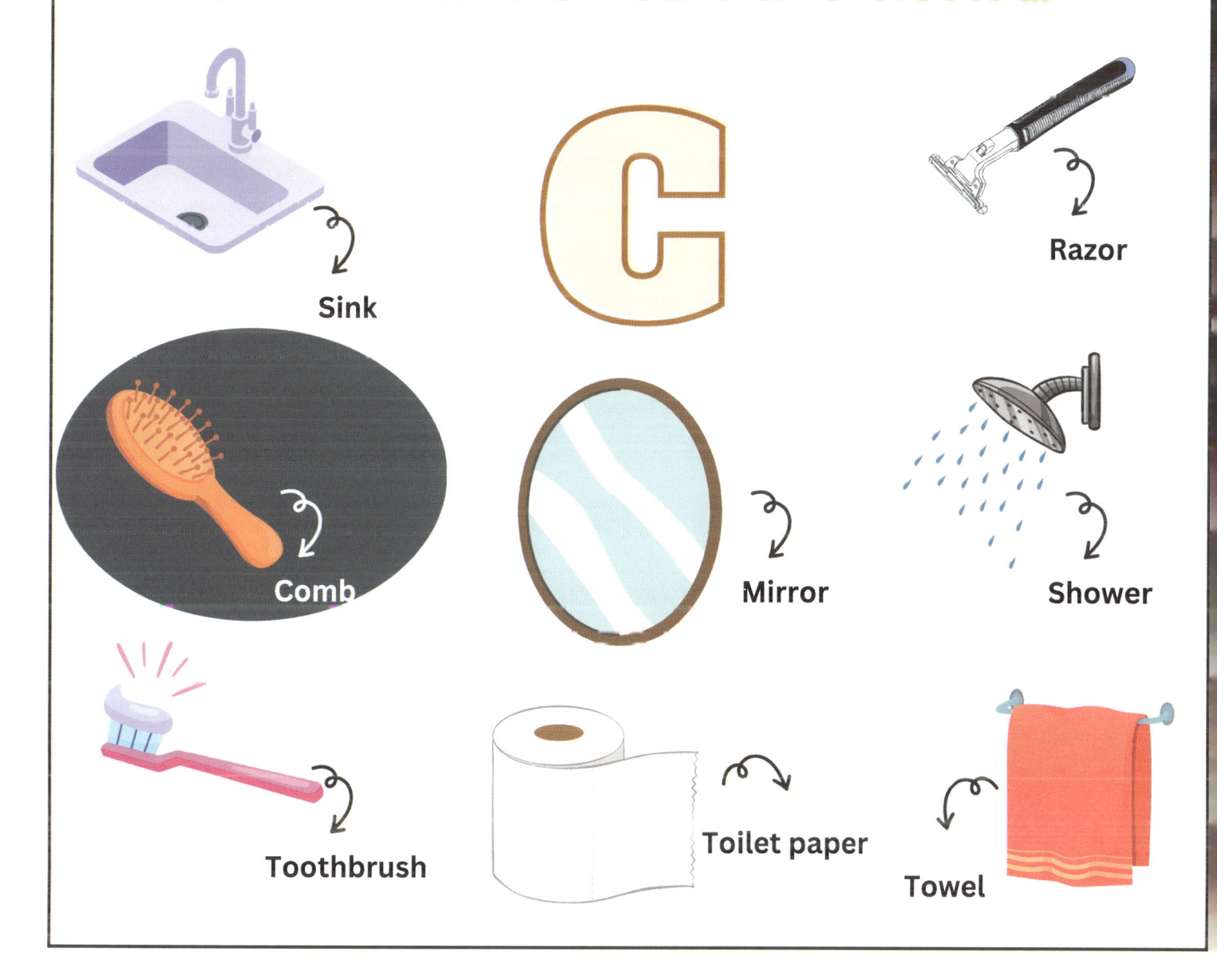

I SPY WITH MY LITTLE EYES SOMETHING BEGINNING WITH ...

C

- Sink
- Razor
- Comb
- Mirror
- Shower
- Toothbrush
- Toilet paper
- Towel

I SPY WITH MY LITTLE EYES SOMETHING BEGINNING WITH ...

C

I SPY WITH MY LITTLE EYES SOMETHING BEGINNING WITH ...

A

- Centipede
- Ant
- Grasshopper
- Bee
- Ladybug
- Dragonfly
- Butterfly
- Mantis
- Snail
- Worm

I SPY WITH MY LITTLE EYES SOMETHING BEGINNING WITH ...

A

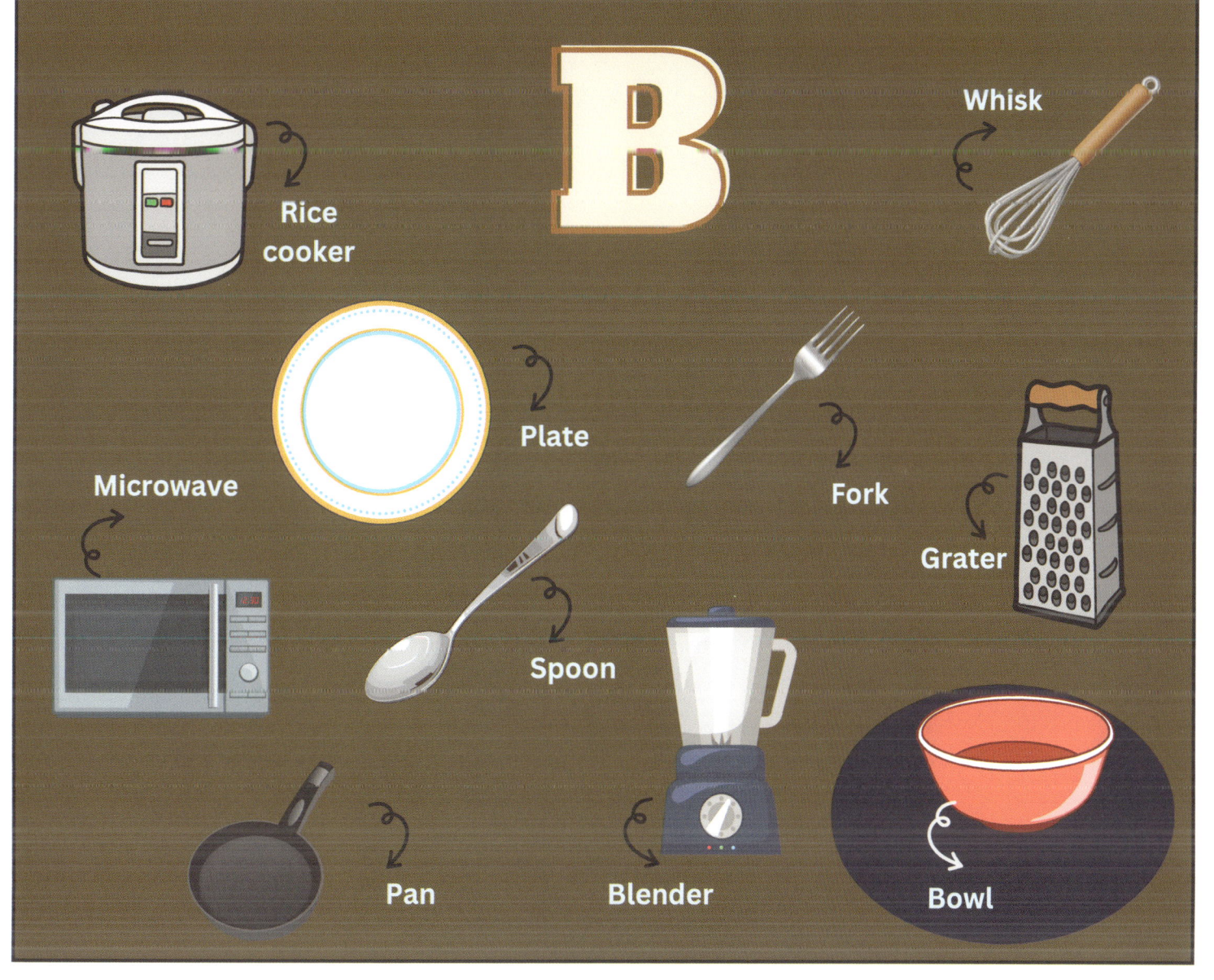

I SPY WITH MY LITTLE EYES SOMETHING BEGINNING WITH ...

B

- Rice cooker
- Whisk
- Plate
- Fork
- Microwave
- Grater
- Spoon
- Pan
- Blender
- Bowl

I SPY WITH MY LITTLE EYES SOMETHING BEGINNING WITH ...

B

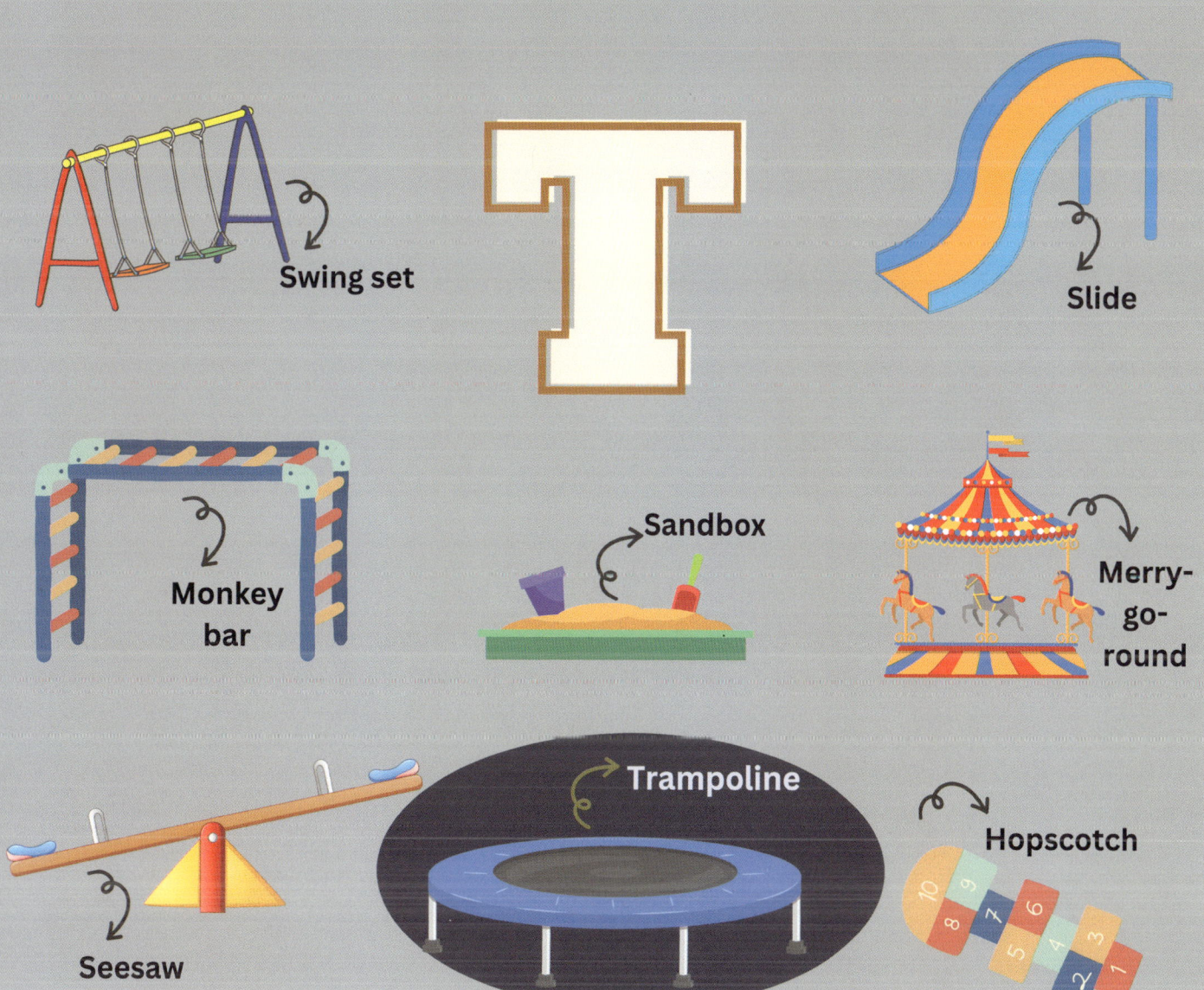

I SPY WITH MY LITTLE EYES SOMETHING BEGINNING WITH ...

T

- Swing set
- Slide
- Monkey bar
- Sandbox
- Merry-go-round
- Seesaw
- Trampoline
- Hopscotch

I SPY WITH MY LITTLE EYES SOMETHING BEGINNING WITH ...

T

I SPY WITH MY LITTLE EYES SOMETHING BEGINNING WITH ...

L

- Television
- Sofa
- Clock
- Plant
- Curtain
- Lamp
- Book
- Carpet
- Coffee table

I SPY WITH MY LITTLE EYES SOMETHING BEGINNING WITH ...

L

3 scorpions

3 lizards

1 vulture

Find the following animals:

2 camels

4 spiders

3 meerkats

2 hippos

2 cheetahs

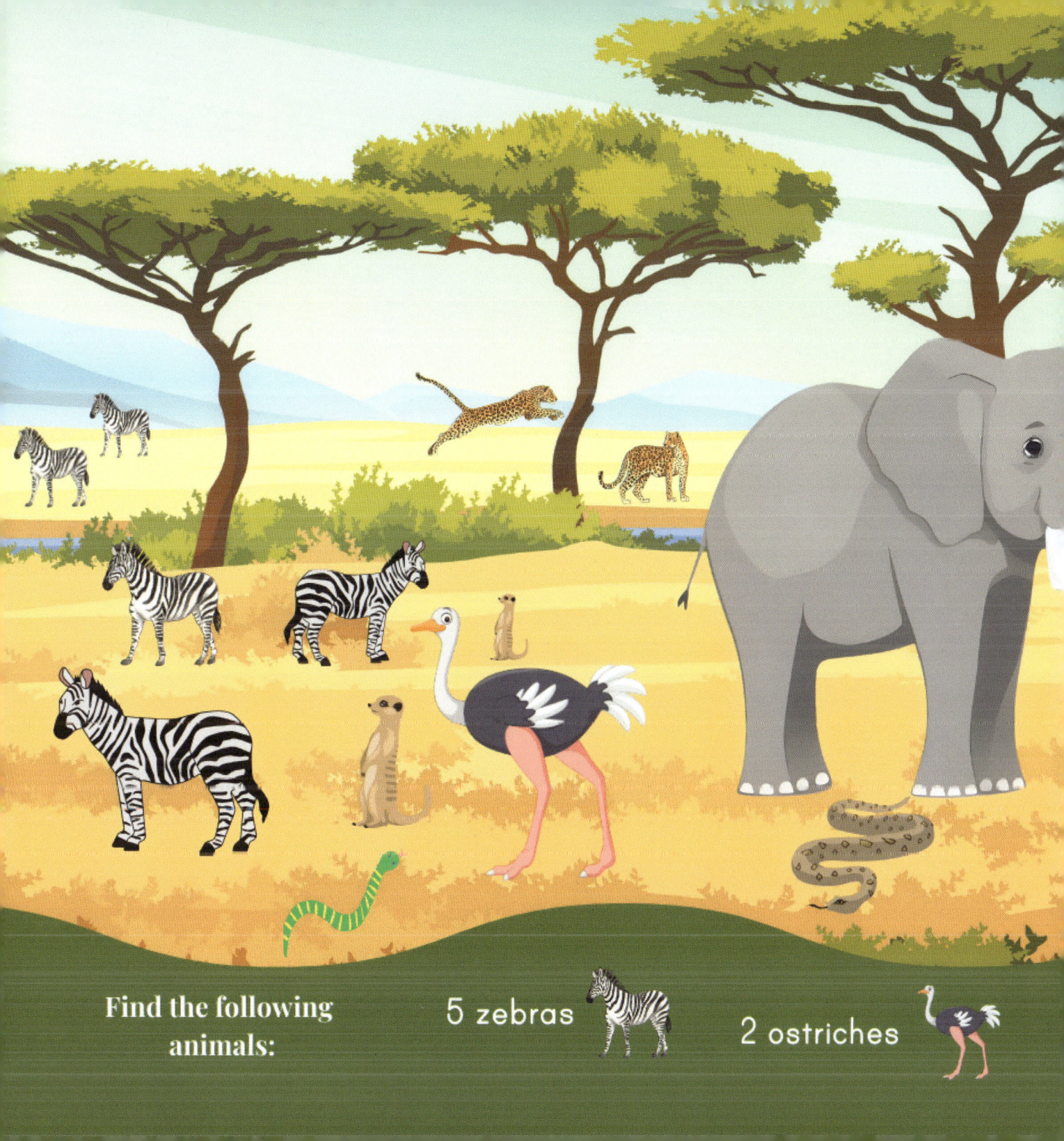

Find the following animals: 5 zebras   2 ostriches

1 shark
2 jelly fish
3 octopuses

Find the following animals: 3 clownfish 2 pufferfish 4 seahorses

3 birds 2cat 2 dairy cows

Find the following animals:

3 pigs

4 goats

5 sheeps

2 coconuts

2 surfboards

5 starfish

Find the following things / animals: 3 monkeys   3 crabs   1 kite

2 fish   3 butterflies   4 frogs

Find the following animals:

1 snake
1 pelican
5 ants

2 ladybugs   3 snails   4 grasshoppers

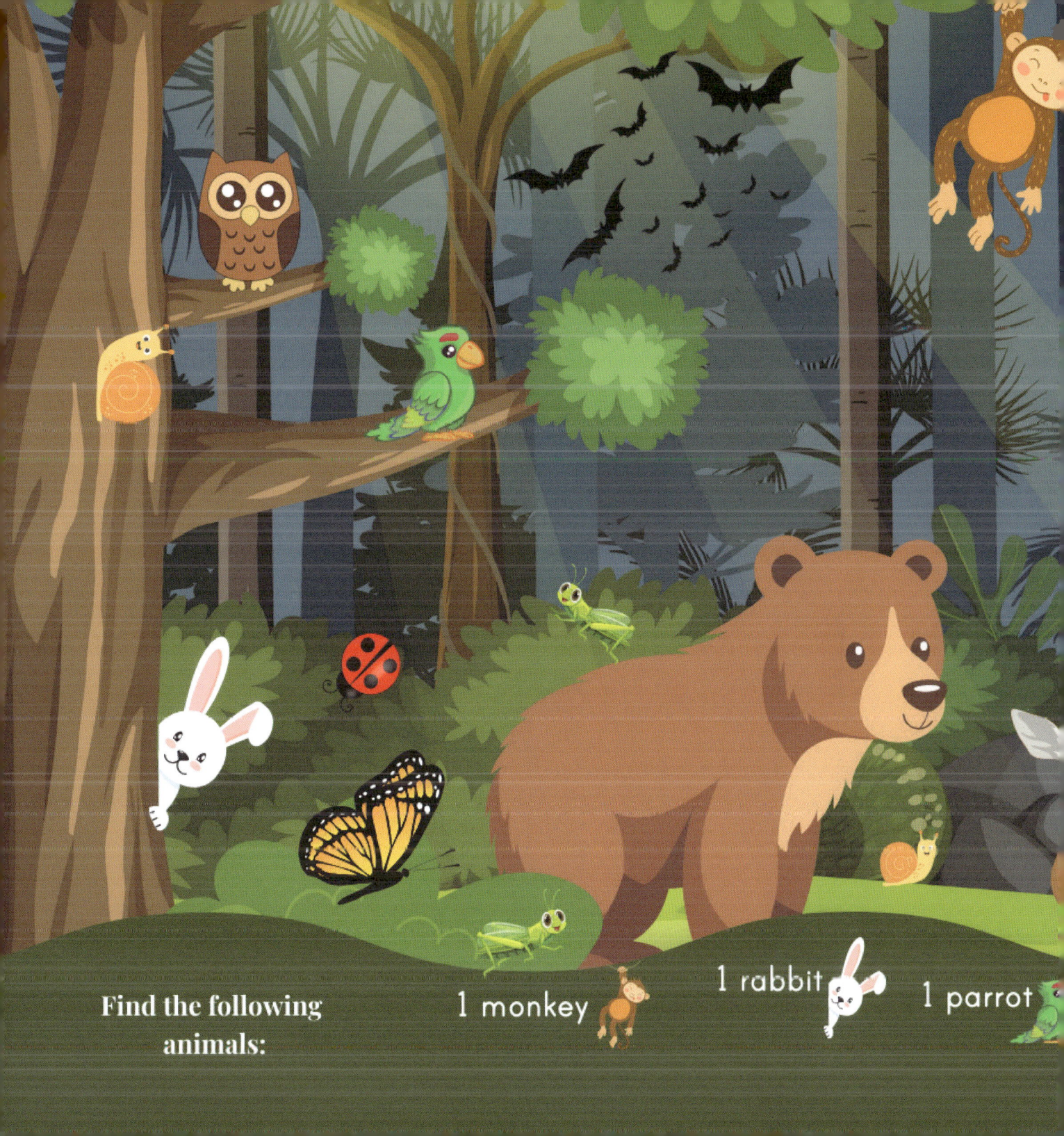

Find the following animals: 1 monkey   1 rabbit   1 parrot

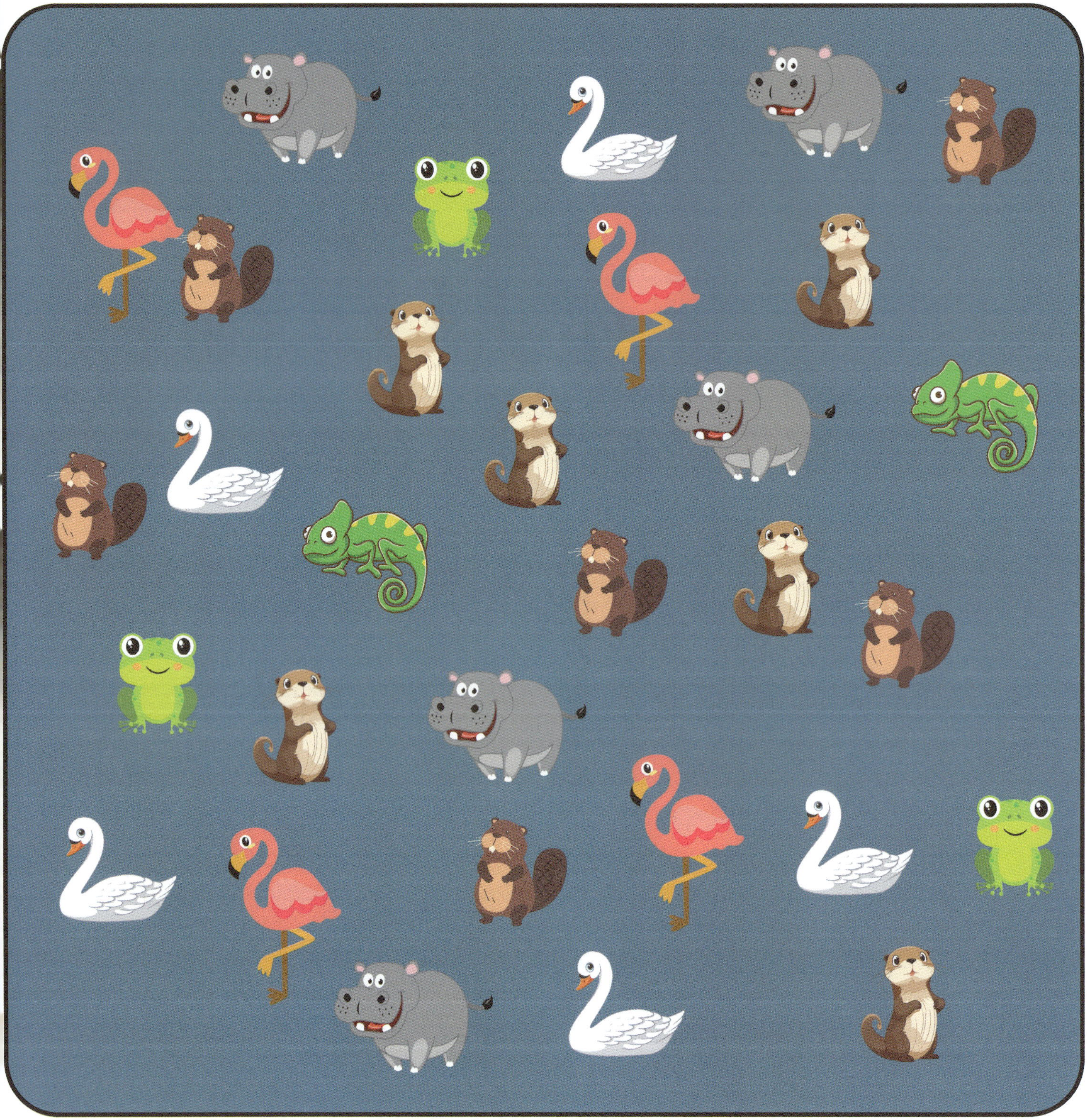

I SPY WITH MY LITTLE EYES...

3 green frogs

5 white swans

6 brown beaver

4 pink flamingoes

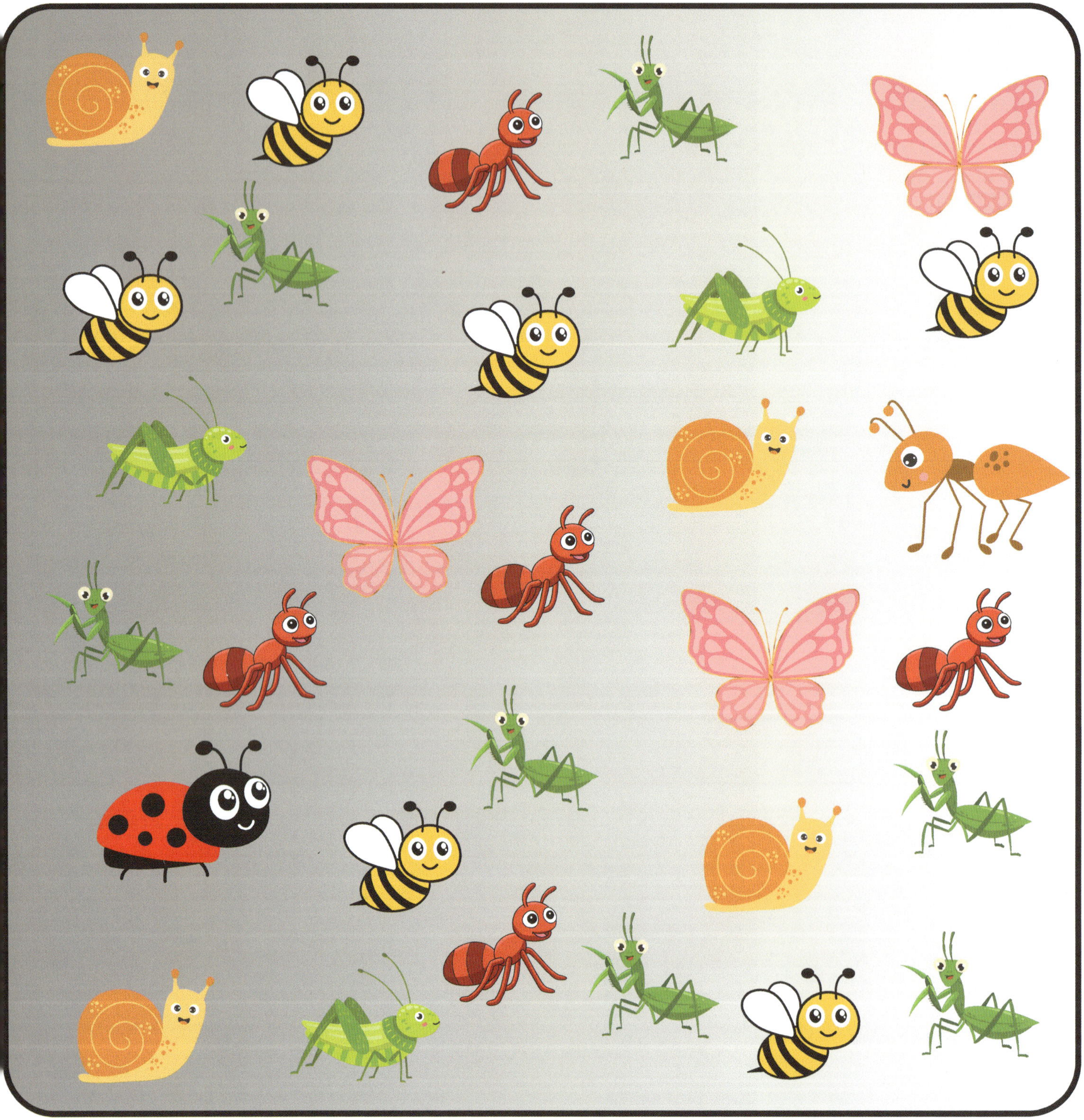

I SPY WITH MY LITTLE EYES...

5 red ants

7 green mantes

6 yellow bees

3 pink butterflies

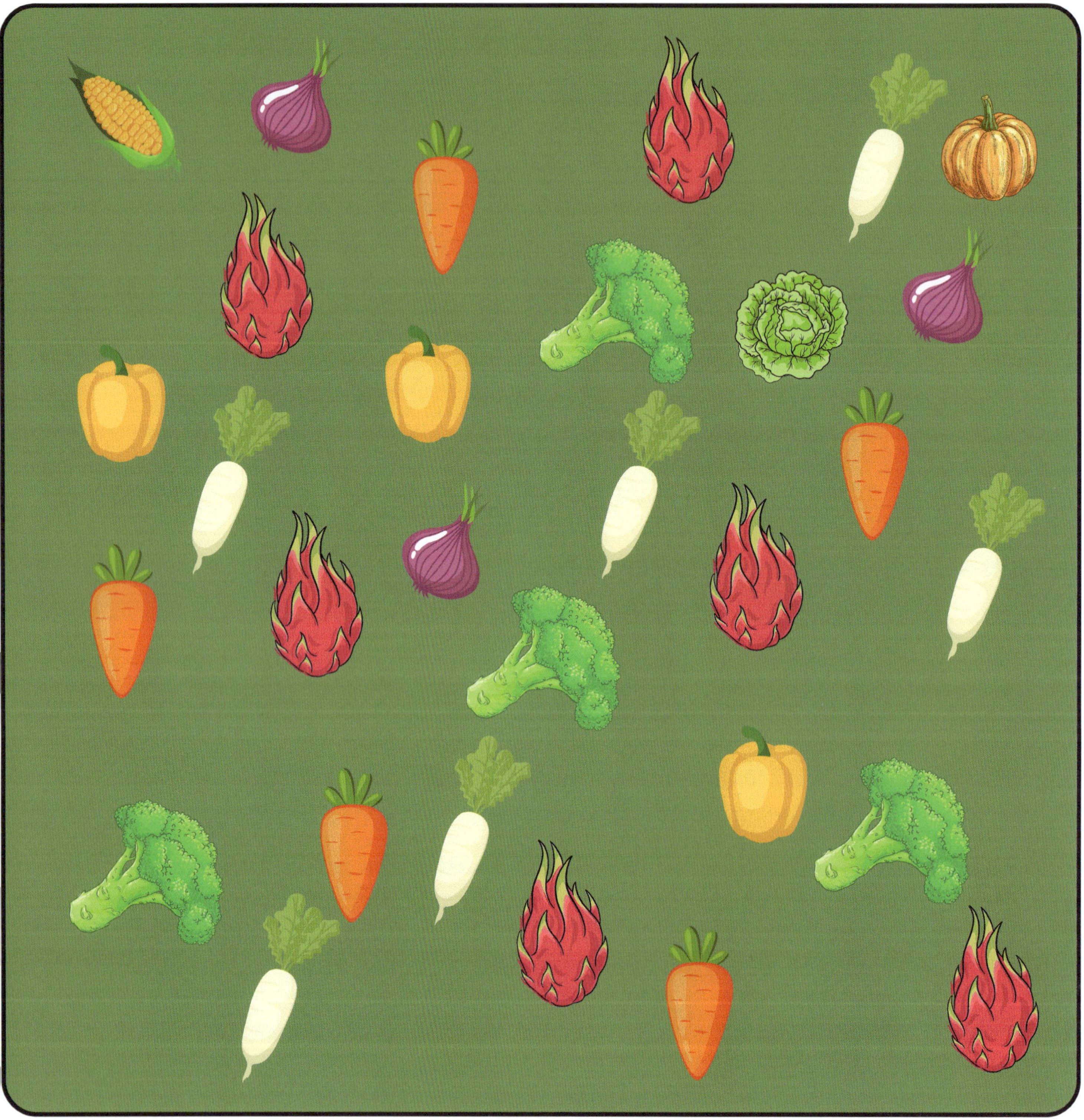

I SPY WITH MY LITTLE EYES...

5 orange carrots

4 green broccali

3 yellow bell peppers

6 pink dragonfruit

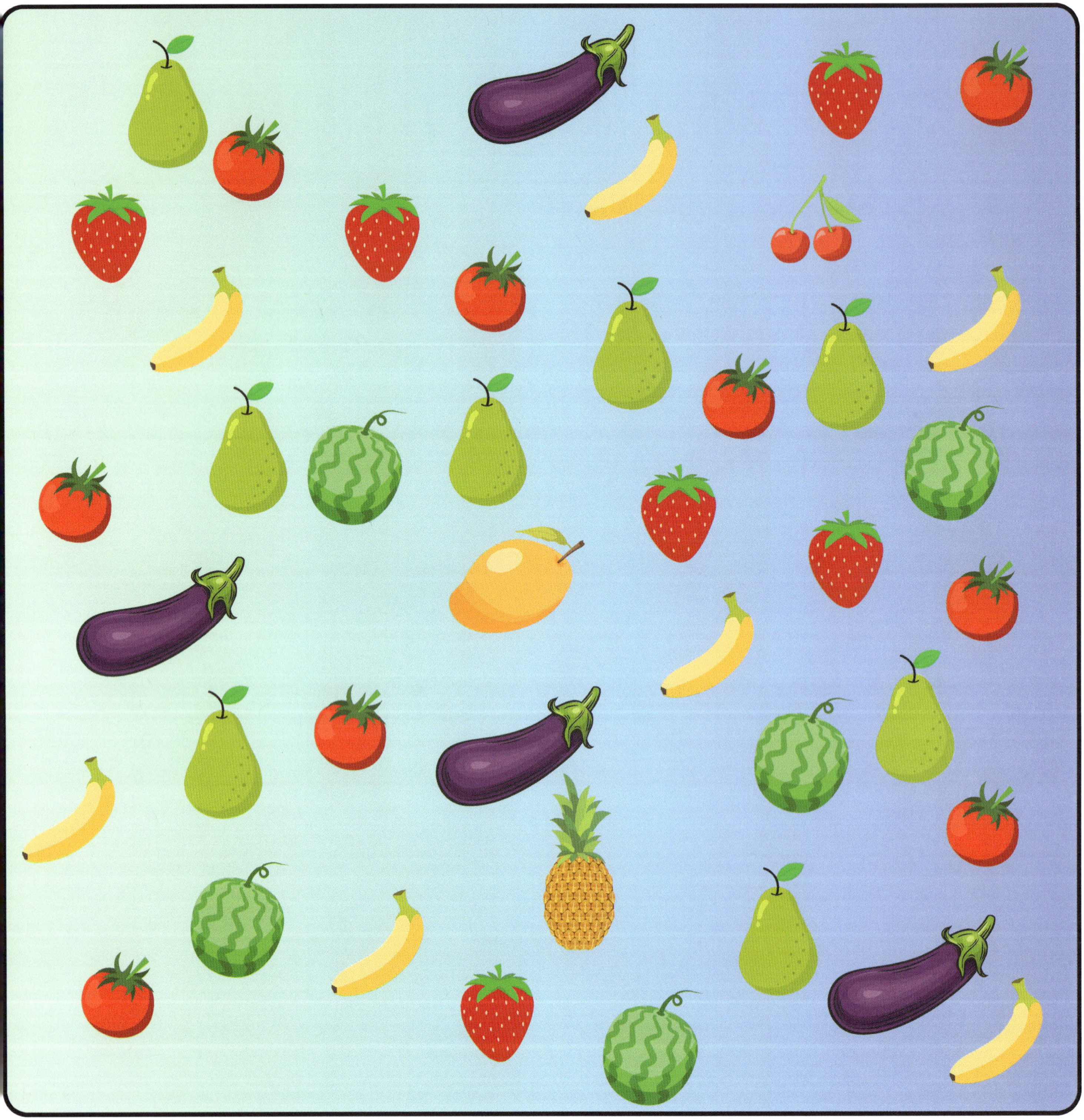

I SPY WITH MY LITTLE EYES...

4 purple eggplants 🍆

5 green watermelons 🍉

9 red tomatoes 🍅

7 yellow bananas 🍌

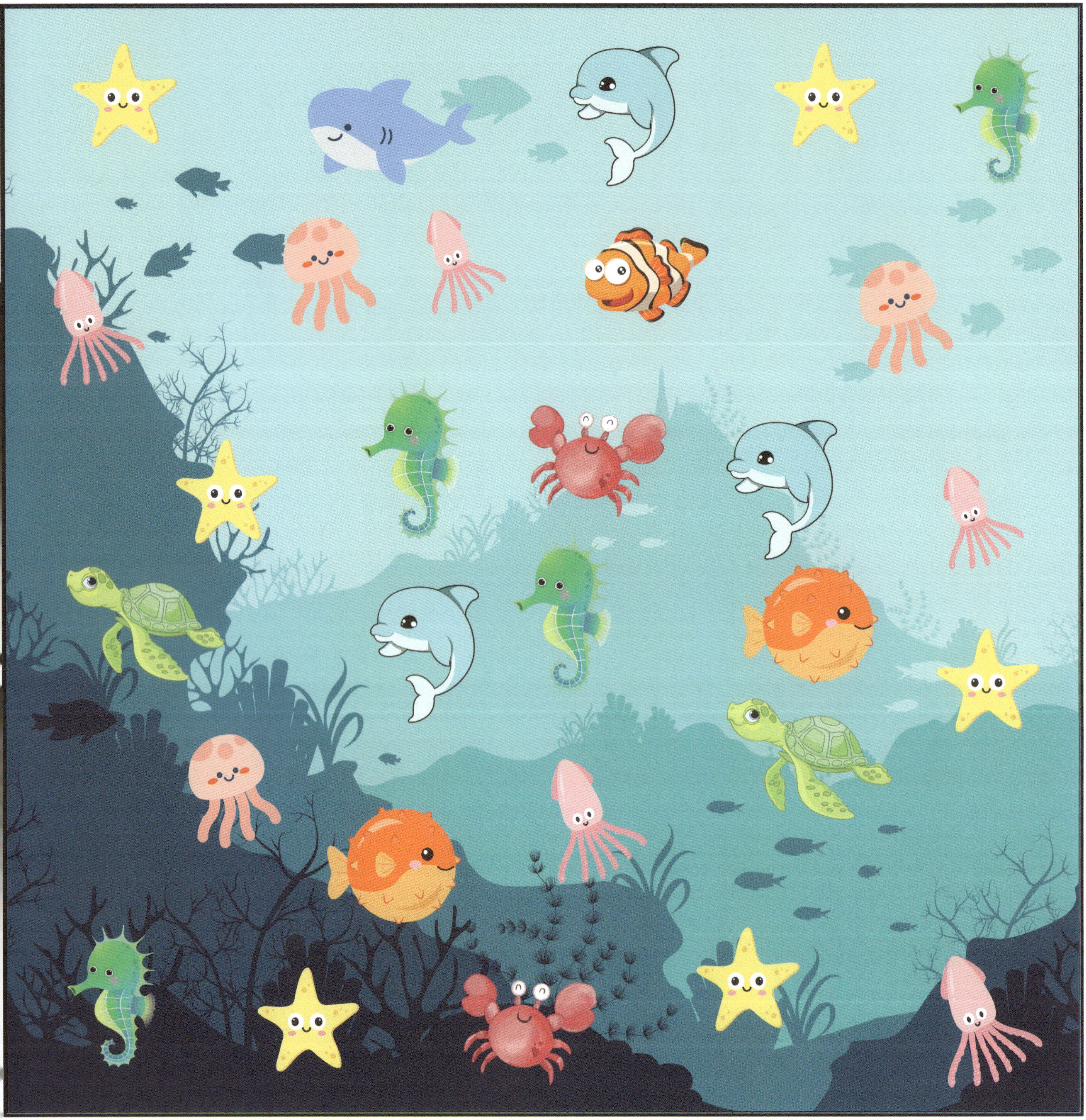

Printed in Great Britain
by Amazon

44053242R00025